Monee' Speaks.
A Spoken Word,
 Speaking Word

By Monee' Rease

Copyright © 2022 Monee' Rease

All rights reserved.

ISBN: 9798387078606

All rights reserved. No part of this publication may be reproduced, stored in retrieval system, or transmitted in any form or by any means- electronic, mechanical, photocopy, recording or otherwise without written permission from the author. Email contact: Moneespeaks@gmail.com

Book Cover design by Breiana Addison
Addison Graphics
Addison.graphics@yahoo.com

Editing: A.T. Destiny Awaits Group LLC
atdestinyawaitsgroup@gmail.com

MY DEDICATION
*REVEALING VALUABLE PIECES OF ME,
WHILE DEDICATING IT TO THE
RELATABLE YOU.*

I never felt heard or as if I had a voice. Writing became my way of speaking, but who was I speaking to, who was listening, or was it that no one understood my language?

As a little one, I'd write and then burn my pages because I didn't want to be chastised or disciplined for what I felt, saw, and or heard, yet I'd expressed on paper—raised to believe that children should be seen and not heard. Voiceless, but my word says, and a child shall lead them.

Silenced by force, not by choice. This routine of muteness turned me into a habitual silencer as I became an adult. Refusing to share my dreams, my visions, my gift of writing etc.... Not wanting to share that part of my life due to fear. That was until my words were discovered. Now I'm being told that I must share because I'm a speaking spirit with power, so speak! Fear gripped my throat even tighter. I was convinced that no one wanted to hear what I needed to share, so

MONEE' SPEAKS,
A SPOKEN WORD, SPEAKING WORD

I remained quiet.

Actively attending service but ineffectively working because I'm quietly sitting on my gift. I've now become a permanent visitor. Fear led me to believe that I'd dodged that bullet of speaking. Little did I know God had assigned a pusher. Someone who wasn't afraid to tell me, "Just because you refuse to do your assignment, I will do and complete mine in your life. You will speak".

It was at that moment, with tears streaming I had to ask God why? Why now? My words never mattered before. No one has ever listened. I'm afraid. He had me do research on my middle name. I later found out that Monee' (Monet') means "to be heard." He was letting me know that my voice mattered.

So, to everyone that has ever felt silenced, unheard, ignored, and or voiceless, this book is dedicated to you. You are a speaking spirit with power, so speak!

Always & Forever,
Monee' Rease

CONTENTS

Acknowledgements..................i

The Blood..................1

Beautifully Flawed..................6

Black Sheep..................10

Birth..................13

Bondage..................17

Conditions..................22

Connection vs Attachment..................25

Correction..................28

Depression..................31

Diseased 1..................34

Love..................38

Order..................41

PEMDAS..................47

MONEE' SPEAKS, A SPOKEN WORD, SPEAKING WORD

Reflection 52

Release 55

Self Esteem 62

Self-Identity 67

Spiritual Sepsis 71

The Chase 74

The Conversation 78

The Garment 81

Who Am I? 84

Worth 89

ACKNOWLEDGMENTS

First, I'd like to thank my heavenly Father for trusting me with the gift of writing. Trusting me to write what I hear, see, and or experience, be it good, bad, or indifferent. Knowing that my heart being on display would expose or give another being the opportunity to embrace your love as I have. Father, I thank you for deliverance, healing, and guidance. I thank you for My Freedom Papers. Father, I thank you in advance for every soul that this book comes in contact with.

To my family, thank you for your love and support throughout my life. I am who I am today because of the lessons you've instilled in me. I appreciate every push. I pray God blesses each of you tremendously.

To my Heir's of The Kingdom Church International Leaders, Vincent T. Warren, Royal, and Alma Scott and Family, thank you for literally loving the hell out of me. When I shifted to the ministry, my assignment was to heal. I didn't know what that would look like as I had to erase *everything, I thought I knew. Full of fear but told I had the freedom papers in my hands. All I had to do was write and speak what God had given me. Thank you for always pushing, supporting, believing in, and seeing me as God does. Never letting me forget that I am a Speaking Spirit with Power, so speak.*

To Verlydia Royal, thank you for pushing and guiding me on this project. I'm truly grateful for our connection. There were many days I wanted to quit but God. Thank you for creating a safe space, unifying a sisterhood with Christian Girl's Rock. I'm honored to be a member.

To Tyeshia Thomas (A.T. Destiny Awaits Group LLC) and Breiana Addison (Addison Graphics), thank you for helping to bring the vision to fruition. I truly appreciate both of you.

To every Leader, Ministry, and Event Planner that has ever invited me to share the Ministry of Monee' Speaks by way of A Spoken Word, I say thank you as well. Every platform has helped to encourage and push me to my next level.

The Blood

MONEE' SPEAKS,
A SPOKEN WORD, SPEAKING WORD

"The Blood"

She was only 5 when her innocence was taken. Plagued by the nightmares that this traumatic act had created. She kept silent as she had been told. Open your mouth, and my wrath will unfold. God, she was only 5! How could this be?! Baby dolls, laughing and giggling...Just being a child, playing innocently.

This was no more. You see, the seed of pain had been planted by an adult with no remorse. Though her physical wounds did heal...the pain in her heart was so great that she didn't want to live. At 5, what does a child know about suicide? Nothing you say? Well, in the act leading up to this she was told to hide. With no one to turn to, she took on the spirit of pride. Even at this age, she knew what had happened wasn't right, but the fear and the words expressed on that night *could cost her, her life.*

She had already been taught that releasing tears meant you were weak. Slowly she began to change, and now she no longer speaks. I love you, she said. You're my favorite, all while being groomed and treated as if it was a man she was dating. Afraid to say anything. I repeated her words in my head... You love me? I'm... your favorite? Little girls love to hear these words.. except what she was doing to me; I hated it!!

Yes, you heard right, I said I. Convinced that I did something wrong, and it was all my fault. She laughed in my face and said, "I'll NEVER GET CAUGHT." I was mute, but the voices in my head grew louder and louder. Go get a razor, put it to your wrist you're better off dead you won't be missed. In my closet crying with blood running down my hand. I was only 5, God, is this really your plan?!

I screamed and screamed, and no one came. Again, the voice said YOU WILL ALWAYS BE THE ONE TO BLAME. I turned the corner, relieved to see my mom. She asked what the explicit are you screaming for? I showed her my wrist. She looked at me, threw her hands up, and angrily said get a towel and get this mess up! And just like that, I was dismissed. I got a towel and began to wipe with tears running down my little face. I cried all night.

I didn't understand, they told me they loved me, but no one told me that love would turn around and hurt me. I grabbed a pillow and retreated to my closet, as this was my safe haven. With the blood-soaked towel, I covered myself and tried to pretend that when I woke up, I'd be in a fairyland. Thirty-five years later and God said here's the

MONEE' SPEAKS,
A SPOKEN WORD, SPEAKING WORD

revelation. The night you covered yourself with the towel you didn't understand that it was blood-stained. No Pain, No Power! It is My DNA running through your veins. That night you bled out, I felt your pain. It was I who came and saved you, though you were hurt. The moral of this story, THE BLOOD STILL WORKS!

Beautifully Flawed

MONEE' SPEAKS,
A SPOKEN WORD, SPEAKING WORD
"Beautifully Flawed"

Beautifully Flawed "Puzzle"

In the process of making the chocolate puzzle pieces, I noticed some of them had discrepancies/flaws that I really didn't like. I began to re-melt or remold some of them, and before I knew it, I had destroyed most of the work that I'd done.

God said, Stop! No one is perfect. All have flaws or have been flawed...but as I've told you in the past, they're still usable. They'll still fit. I wouldn't have initially had you paint them gold if they weren't of value. Flawed but favored, flawed but functional, flawed and free. BEAUTIFULLY FLAWED!

Flawed doesn't mean unusable. It simply means you survived the process, and your scars are a testament to the healing that's taken place. BEAUTIFULLY FLAWED!

Don't throw away what you've deemed unusable or ugly because that's the beauty of your pain. Puzzle pieces are broken individually; however, when connected correctly, they'll fulfill their purpose of producing a bigger picture. Every piece matters and is equally important. BEAUTIFULLY FLAWED!

The world says, "I'll do it when I get myself together." That day will never come because you can't do it alone. They'll have you trying to recreate or fit into a mold that was never intended for you. Try putting the puzzle together without your piece...because being out of position will create a void, a hole...an empty space. Incompleteness, and that's not of Me. Whose purpose would you have helped to abort while out of position or

MONEE' SPEAKS,
A SPOKEN WORD, SPEAKING WORD

conforming to something you're not? Your pieces will not fit every puzzle; however, they're the same size, just cut differently. Identify your pieces within your assigned puzzle: flaws and all. I'm waiting because you're still usable.
BEAUTIFULLY FLAWED!

Black Sheep

MONEE' SPEAKS,
A SPOKEN WORD, SPEAKING WORD

"Black Sheep"

The world's definition of a "Black Sheep" is a member of a family or group who is regarded as a disgrace to them. "Black" means strength, authority, importance, and power. While "Sheep" are defined as followers of Christ. How can two words be presented as powerful in a single sense but, when combined have a negative meaning? We've gone from being sheep to being "the goat."

The "Greatest Of All Time," He was/is the greatest, yet He wasn't a Goatherder. He was a "Shepherd." He had/has followers. Sheep follow; goats choose not to. A group of goats are known as a trip, and that's exactly what the world is doing "Trippen!" You can't take the strength and power of a true follower and deem it something negative. No longer will I look at the Black Sheep as being a powerless *disgrace but rather a strong authoritative figure who follows Christ.*

Birth

MONEE' SPEAKS, A SPOKEN WORD, SPEAKING WORD
"Birth"

I was taught to believe that birth was something every woman should be able to give. The only problem with this lesson was if it didn't happen physically, it wasn't considered real. As a little girl, I'd dream and fantasize about my wedding. Us picking out the house together, depending on the baby's we'd create. Never could I imagine that this wasn't my fate.

The first time I heard it, I was only 19... Ms. Rease, I apologize and understand your pain but giving birth shall never be. I pushed this news to the back of my head, not wanting to deal with this.. Why bother? I already felt dead. My mother produced 4, but 3 survived. Me being the only girl, I wouldn't dare tell her my womb wouldn't thrive. I was under pressure, and because they didn't understand *me, they put me in a box and labeled me anything but what God called me. Depression, anger, and rage is what I felt, which led to multiple suicide attempts. Pills plus drinking so that I could sleep. Deep down inside, I knew this wasn't me but no matter what my soul wanted my flesh was weak.*

For years I cried over this, and no one knew until baby girl walked in the room one night and said Mommy, what's wrong with you? Yes, I'm a mommy so let me back up. It was in that moment that I realized I was being selfish and had life messed up.

See, at 15, God gifted me with a 3-day-old little cutee. Dark curly hair, dimples, and turned-in feet. From that moment forward, my child she would always be. I was so selfish that I hadn't realized that my dreams of being a mother didn't require me to labor. Baby girl entered my life pain-free.

MONEE' SPEAKS,
A SPOKEN WORD, SPEAKING WORD

Don't tell me that isn't favor!

At an early age, I made it known what my desires for my seed would look like, and oh have I sown. I remember looking at her little face, and it was love at first sight. One round of prayer, YES, I got it right! My baby wasn't birth from my womb but created and birth from my heart.

See my heart is the dwelling place of Jesus. If He resides there, what better place to give birth? The place where love should always be, abound. Little did I know God was working on my heart and turning things around. Baby girl was my blessing in disguise. I would love, cherish and pray she'd be wise. As years went by and baby girl grew, I heard God say... She was birth into your life to save you from you.

MONEE' SPEAKS,
A SPOKEN WORD, SPEAKING WORD

BONDAGE

MONEE' SPEAKS,
A SPOKEN WORD, SPEAKING WORD

"Bondage"

You would think that the first rule of the house would be to love God. Not where I come from... God was never mentioned, but if you shift your eyes to the left in the corner where multiple switches... just waiting for you to break the "Golden Rule." You know, one that says what goes on in my house... stays in my house. Well, Ummm excuse me, Sir, can you serve me an eviction?

This statement causes more damage than it's worth. Taught me to be invisible. Pain is only safe if it's hidden. My first lesson...2 years old and slapped in the mouth and told, "Stop Telling My Business." All I could do was cry. I'm still a baby. Do you not understand I'm imitating you? Don't like what I'm saying, then change what you do! Of course, I'm told to stay in a child's place. I'm a fast learner... lesson of the day "stay quiet; it's safe."

I took this lesson everywhere I went. Chauncey, do you have something to say? Me, open my mouth! Oh, you got me bent...I knew what I was going home to. It was deeply drilled in my head. "Tell if you want to. When they bring you back... trust I got you."

Every home is a house, but every house isn't a home. Cut MY light off... close MY refrigerator... shut MY door... everything was possessive! Everything was yours. Now I'm uncomfortable because I never asked to be here. I never asked to be born. Seems like everything you possess, you love, except what you birthed; I'm yours.

I heard MY before every command except when it came to taking out the

MONEE' SPEAKS,
A SPOKEN WORD, SPEAKING WORD

trash. Do you not see this? TAKE THE TRASH OUT! As I gathered the bag and said very low... What happened to the MY? This is yours too. You've never owned your trash but put it off on me as if I've said more bondage, please!

This house holds a lot of secrets. Abuse of every kind, but I dare not share... because that premature death certificate wasn't going to be mine.

I'm getting older and longing for the day I move out... at any moment, chaos was subject to break out. A minute situation always made grand. Let's line up; which one of us will the abuse land? I brought you in this world, and I'll take you out. Now me in my head again...umm, Sir, you're not my father. He got up in my face and said, "I'll kill you and that ------. I don't care about you being another man's daughter. It was as if he heard my *thoughts. Fear would lead to begging and pleading... for we all knew what was coming next.*

You see because those on the outside looking in saw a different version of the people I lived with. That time has come. I'm 18. My dreams of wanting to be free await me. Only thing is I wasn't free. I was taunted by the hidden things of my past. You know the secrets that be. Even in my own space, I still carried their trash. "What goes on in my house, stays in my house"... will create a mark that will last.

Damaged goods, but I'll give myself the gift of freedom as God has said...I CAN STILL BE USED.

Conditions

MONEE' SPEAKS,
A SPOKEN WORD, SPEAKING WORD

"Conditions'

Unconditional is a word many get confused with conditional. Conditions are great except when it comes to love. Conditions will have you acting out of your emotions or being fake based on your current need of a person or thing.

See, conditions will eventually backfire. Leaving your heart in a state that you've left others feeling...broken, used, hurt etc...wait! What happens when your pain is self-inflicted? When you know, you've loved unconditionally? So, you thought. You've loved on and nurtured everyone else but the one person who needed you the most. Confused? Well, go look in the mirror. Do you now see the state of the condition you're in? The unconditional love that you gave others... you didn't feel worthy enough to give yourself. They're having fun,

MONEE' SPEAKS,
A SPOKEN WORD, SPEAKING WORD

and your heart is barely FUNctioning.

Oh, My child, you've married everyone else and their issues all while dating yourself. You haven't gotten your ring because you've gotten into the ring with them to fight a battle that wasn't yours to fight. While they feel that they've won...this has left you down for the count. Unable to move causing you to throw in the towel. Why? When victory was yours from the beginning. Yes, I told you to shake the dust off of your feet, but I never said let the dirt weigh you down. Get up! Let go, but yet hold on!! Your condition is about to become unconditional.

MONEE' SPEAKS,
A SPOKEN WORD, SPEAKING WORD

Connection vs Attachment...

MONEE' SPEAKS,
A SPOKEN WORD, SPEAKING WORD

"Connection vs Attachment..."

Connection vs Attachment...

The doors will be opened but be very careful of who you embrace or allow to enter, as anyone can be a part of your life, but not everyone can or should be a part of your spirit. There's a difference in a connection vs. an attachment. One activates or gives power; the other depletes your life.

Have you ever heard anyone say I'm going to attach myself to God? No, because most only speak of being connected. When talking about My power and what's been implanted by Me within you... I've stated that I've given you power. You have to want to be connected to receive power. Just as the TV plug has to be connected to the *power socket, otherwise it's useless. When the plug meets the power source, you can then change the channel as you so desire. Change will not happen without power! It's the same way with Me... when the plug (you) meets the power source (Me) things will begin to change for your good... you're now POWERFUL...*

The enemy knows all too well that you see him. He's determined to make you question every God-ordained relationship (connection) because he has failed with attachment. Attachment isn't you, you don't get that close... so he'll try to make a connection appear as an attachment which will attempt to cause you to back up...remember you are a source that's needed. Someone is waiting for your power.

MONEE' SPEAKS,
A SPOKEN WORD, SPEAKING WORD

Correction

MONEE' SPEAKS,
A SPOKEN WORD, SPEAKING WORD
"Correction"

This word came after an unintentional mistake...I don't want to get into what transpired.

God had me to go buy two different types of ink pens. One with permanent ink and the other with erasable ink..the permanent pen represents man..no matter the mistake you make, be it intentional or unintentional, they won't let you live it down. You can apologize, and yet some still won't allow you to move past your mistakes. It's permanent with them. Then you have the erasable pen that represents God...the eraser is repentance (apology). Once you've apologized, it's forgiven...erased,gone...done. He doesn't hold it against you....but what do you do when you've apologized with a sincere heart, and yet it's still an *issue? God says that's when I come in with white out. I'll blot out or purify the situation, and if they choose to hold on to it... you've been released from it. You've done your part. Destiny doesn't end with disconnection...I disconnect what isn't Destined. Erased and purified... There's always a fresh start with God.*

MONEE' SPEAKS,
A SPOKEN WORD, SPEAKING WORD

Depression

MONEE' SPEAKS,
A SPOKEN WORD, SPEAKING WORD
"Depression"

Why do ya'll allow the world to give status on your atmosphere? If the meteorologist states that ya'll are about to face a tropical depression instantly, it is believed. Tropical means hot, oppressive, or heavy. Yet ya'll wonder why no one is being healed or delivered from depression. The world has yet dressed it up, and ya'll have accepted it.

The meteorologist can declare depression throughout the airwaves, and it's ok, but I died for your peace, freedom, and sins...yet most still don't believe anything I've said. The warning of a storm and to the store you'll go. The warning of eternal life in hell, and it's ignored. Where are my atmosphere changers? The meteorologist has a job, true enough, but do you know their employer? Who

MONEE' SPEAKS,
A SPOKEN WORD, SPEAKING WORD

do you work for or believe in? What's your forecast? What will you speak or declare? Will you command/charge the atmosphere?

MONEE' SPEAKS,
A SPOKEN WORD, SPEAKING WORD

Diseased 1

MONEE' SPEAKS,
A SPOKEN WORD, SPEAKING WORD

"Diseased 1"

Are you Diseased, or are you Dis-Eased? Trust there's a difference between the two. See, too often, we don't want to deal with the real us. Especially those holding a title. We believe we got it all together & nothing can affect us. We lift our hands, throw our heads back, jerk a little bit & will even speak in tongues, but when this habitual routine is over, our stench begins to seep; The stench of judgment, jealousy, backbiting, control, and gossiping just to name a few...

See, these are spiritually transmitted diseases. Your infection is about to be revealed! You won't examine yourself before poisoning His seeds. By His stripes, He said that you were healed, but you've chosen to ignore His word. You opened your mouth and bombed another soul you've *killed! Yeah, there goes that tongue again.*

See your disease is causing His people to be dis-eased in the body of Christ. You use your platform or opportunities to speak what thus said self & not what He, Himself, has spoken to you. It comes out like word vomit! You're supposed to be PRAYING, but instead, you're too busy PREYING on His people like leeches & this has caused Him to be Dis-eased. He's bothered. He wants harmony & you're causing harm. He wants ease & you're creating a spiritual disease.

Your world has never been about Him. Yes, you have followers, but they're too blind to see where it is that you're leading them. You've gotten caught up in what man can do for you instead of what you can do for Him. Your trinity has even changed. No longer the Father, Son & Holy Ghost;

MONEE' SPEAKS,
A SPOKEN WORD, SPEAKING WORD

now it's all about me, myself & I. What's the matter?! You grab your chest... the first sign of a spiritual heart attack. Keep it up, and you will surely die! You never stopped to think that you would be affected...oh you thought the symptoms were only for those you infected? Naw, that's not the way things go ... apparently, you've forgotten you reap what you sow. Consider this a warning and get yourself together. You can't kill what I spoke to and said live.

MONEE' SPEAKS,
A SPOKEN WORD, SPEAKING WORD

Love

MONEE' SPEAKS, A SPOKEN WORD, SPEAKING WORD

"Love"

Love...four letters that are often misused because we have yet to understand that it requires action. Love is a movement or operation. Not just a word to be reciprocated without effort.

You see...Christ was and still is love. Oh, what a love! He came into this cruel world with the understanding that in the end, it would be His life for yours. Who on this earth, in this present moment, would carry your sinfulness and truly lay down their life for yours? He was sin free! He did nothing wrong! Who would do this?! He had a choice, and He chose you. He chose love. He knew what was in His father's Will, and yet men beat, mocked, and even tried to kill what was designed to help us live. If the roles were reversed, would you *remain on that cross? They didn't kill Him. He gave up the ghost, but if this was your option today, would you run and get ghost?*

The greatest gift to man isn't found under a tree or in a stocking. It's found in the ability to love as Christ did and not let His death be in vain. While you're up early Christmas morning unwrapping gifts, can you imagine what Mary felt in the beginning? Her best gift, her firstborn that she wrapped and swaddled as a baby, would now take up His cross and physically leave. You go broke trying to buy gifts. Why when God sent someone to help your brokenness? The Gift was free. It costs you nothing to receive. He didn't say let Me ponder upon the thought nor did He second guess Himself. Actions were taken, and the promise was fulfilled. The Gift of Love yet remains. And again, I say WHAT A LOVE!!

MONEE' SPEAKS,
A SPOKEN WORD, SPEAKING WORD

Order.

MONEE' SPEAKS,
A SPOKEN WORD, SPEAKING WORD

"Order."

ORDER PERIOD "ORDER"

I had a dream that I was in the laundromat. The sign on the washing machine read "broken out of order" due to the knob. The dream continues, and now I'm in my laundry room at home, and I know the knob on my machine is broken. I politely got a pair of pliers and set it to my desired cycle and moved on.

At this point, I began to ask God, is there a difference between broken and brokeness? Because one machine read BROKEN...OUT OF ORDER, and the other was able to function in BROKENNESS; both machines had the same issue, dysfunction or stronghold.

He goes on to show me the laundromat washing machine, a vending machine, and a pay phone. What do they have in common? They all require "change." Keep in mind that He's speaking of the old school equipment. Not the modern-day card readers where you instantly want credit for something, all while bypassing change.

Again, both machines had the same issue, but because this one read broke out of order, you made no effort to insert the change that's required for Me to pre-wash or loosen up the dirt, wash, rinse/purify and spin your situation around.

Change requires effort. You want Me to move, but you won't. You want Me to keep placing you here, doing this and doing that. You have the nerve to have a double standard when it comes to you and I. You wouldn't put your money into a vending machine that reads "out of order" so why do you expect Me to put anything in you when you're out of order? This "Out of order spirit is leaving my house today."

A few Sundays ago, my granddaughter had a meltdown over change. I normally give them a dollar for service. This particular day she wanted change, but I insisted she take the dollar. She cried. I let it go. The next Sunday, another meltdown over change. This time I took her outside and asked her what was her problem? With tears in her eyes, she said Nanna, I just want change. I just want change. Me being serious minded, said...Girl, get yourself together! Instantly I heard God say, "She's trying." What she wants in the physical is what I'm requiring in the spiritual. Change for change, and her spirit understood that. I apologized to her, and she took every coin I had that day and placed it in the bucket. She skipped back to me and said...Nanna change made it all better.

Do you all not realize that that's

the one thing God has been trying to get us to do since this virus started? Change, but we're too busy condemning those who did or didn't take the vaccine. Too busy worrying about where everyone else's faith was. Too busy worrying about everything but what He wanted from us, and that was "change."

It was evident anytime you went into a store; they had signs asking for exact change or a sign that read we're short on change. I read a sign yesterday that said, "please use your debit/credit card because we don't have change." How is it that My children won't change? How is it that you're ok with the Kingdom attempting to be short-changed? How is it?

So again, I ask you, how do you expect Me to put anything in you when you're out of order? This spirit is

MONEE' SPEAKS,
A SPOKEN WORD, SPEAKING WORD

leaving My house today. Change is in Order.

MONEE' SPEAKS,
A SPOKEN WORD, SPEAKING WORD

PEMDAS

MONEE' SPEAKS,
A SPOKEN WORD, SPEAKING WORD

"PEMDAS"

"The Great Divide"

How Bad Do You Want It...

Math helps us to understand patterns and quantify relationships. At some point in school, we learned the order of operations, which is a rule that tells the correct sequence of steps for evaluating a mathematical expression. This expression is called PEMDAS, which means Parenthesis, Exponents, Multiplication, Division Addition, Subtraction...however the acronym for this mathematical technique is Please Excuse My Dear Aunt Sally.

You know, Sis. Sally was lost and confused but didn't know it. She had a lot of excuses for her actions. Let me show you what it looks like in My eyes. I created a woman with a unique strength, and most of you know your *power (for lack of better words, use your imagination). You know what lies between your Parentheses (legs), but yet you keep allowing your Ex or somebody's ex to manipulate your body Multiple times in ungodly ways, only to be Divided with the decision of should I go or should I stay. You stay because he's enticed you and has Added to your heel and wig collection but at the same time Subtracting the very essence of God from your soul.*

See, Sally didn't know her worth. She didn't know she was worth saving. She didn't allow Me to hold and lay hands on her while caressing her heart spiritually. Sally didn't understand that I could make love to her mind and body (all while she's covered), and she would still rise with dignity the next morning. Sally did give into a Will but too bad it wasn't Mine... Now, Will gave her what she wanted, but he wasn't what she needed. It took her awhile to realize that what she thought was free... cost her more than she could afford to lose. She'd lost her dignity, self-respect but most of all, her spiritual identity all because of her belief in man's order of operations or, should I say, the wrong Will. With nothing left to lose, she dropped to her knees and said God, not my will, but Thy Will Be Done!

Sally at that moment realized that in order to truly be happy she had to use PEMDAS in reverse. She had to repent...Subtract every excuse she'd created to satisfy her flesh. She had to release herself from man's order of operations and Add The God of Order. No longer being Divided by the decisions of should I go or should I stay...her spirit of discernment has been Multiplied (strengthened). She has become her own Exponent, which means she believes, promotes, and stands in her power and truth.

MONEE' SPEAKS,
A SPOKEN WORD, SPEAKING WORD

As she started to reverse this thing the enemy began to laugh and rejoice because he believed she was operating in sadness, due to her word being SAD-ME. He moved too fast, didn't realize she still had the letter P left... We all know that the enemy will do anything to keep you distracted from your purpose, your healing, your breakthrough... but with a made-up mind, Sally looked him in the face and sarcastically said...SAD ME PLEASE (NEVER)!!!!

I didn't value the power of Parentheses then, but I do now. Parentheses mean clarification. It is clear that if I stay in the midst of Him, He will surround me. It is clear that everything concerning me will be enclosed in Him. It is clear that He is the beginning and the end...so again, I say to you, SAD, ME PLEASE NEVER!!! Not my will, but His will be done.

MONEE' SPEAKS,
A SPOKEN WORD, SPEAKING WORD

Reflection

MONEE' SPEAKS,
A SPOKEN WORD, SPEAKING WORD

"Reflection"

When they look at you, who will they see? Will it be an image of Myself or a distorted version of a puffed-up man-pleasing fake wanna-be? When I knock on the door of your heart, will you open it and welcome Me? Or slam it shut until you once more have a need... then you seek Me?! When I ask where's My location within you...Will you sit quietly? Or boldly respond...GOD, IN MY SOUL, I CARRY YOU!

See, I knew your responses before I asked, remember, I am God; I created this test. Oh, My child, I am pleased. A vessel that stands before man, but yet it's My reflection they see. One who will give praise and honor that's due because he understands he's called to worship Me in spirit and in truth. No this isn't solely about him but more of

MONEE' SPEAKS,
A SPOKEN WORD, SPEAKING WORD

who resides within him. He gave Me his mess, and I made it work. Oh, did you forget I created Adam from dirt?! When you allow Me to stand up within you as your flesh bows down, I have no choice but to bless your foundation and place upon your head a crown. Most will say favor isn't fair but that night My son gave up His life. Do their actions show they cared? He is who/what I created, so with eyes wide open or close in him, you will find Me, and he is who I chose.

MONEE' SPEAKS,
A SPOKEN WORD, SPEAKING WORD

Release

MONEE' SPEAKS,
A SPOKEN WORD, SPEAKING WORD

"Release"

In 2014 I had a dream about a waterfall. As I was standing next to it, I tried to catch the water. No matter how many times I cupped or repositioned my hands, the water would seep through. Still, I tried again and again and again. Doing the same thing repeatedly and hoping for different results. Trying to make the impossible possible when the message of the dream was "Release, let it go."

I've struggled in this area for years because I never really understood or grasped the concept of letting go of something that wasn't physically in my hands. If I didn't pick it up, how was I supposed to let it go? I didn't understand this spiritually. Sunday after Sunday, I'm at the altar, and someone is in my ear yelling "Just let it go! One Sunday, I screamed back, "How?! I don't understand the instructions." The attachments to the heart and mind are much deeper than you know. I don't even remember how or where I picked it up. I'm trying. I'm here asking for help. We're at the altar, and not one word of prayer was given, not a let's touch and agree...Just a very forceful "Let it go".

I later found out that a discussion was had prior to service. Not only was the information obtained incorrectly. It wasn't even about me, she spoke to the wrong person. This forceful let it go was for something I wasn't holding...so going to the altar became pointless. I'm reading, having dreams and visions, yet I don't understand any of it. The only thing I let go of was my desire to know and understand how to let go of things spiritually. I remained silent, shut down, and two years later, He had me shift.

MONEE' SPEAKS,
A SPOKEN WORD, SPEAKING WORD

He said you will have a release party. Guests and invitations aren't needed as this event only requires the presence of two. I've never had fun in a dream. Most of my dreams/visions are serious, but on Sunday (Sept. 4, 2022) night, I had an explosive amount of fun in my dream. I didn't appear to be pregnant or anything. He smiled at me and then grabbed my hand. Normally He'd ask me...Are you ready? This time He said, "You're Ready." I thought we were about to jump. I inhaled as deep as I could; when I exhaled a massive waterfall began to flow from my stomach. I heard Him say, "That exhale was the push that was needed. Power! Now you understand. Released to release."

Though your flow can't be stopped the party was private and by invitation only. Barriers, dams, plugs, or should I say haters and enemies weren't allowed because when it's time for the body of water to sit (rest), I'll be the drain stopper. I've always held you however, your release date was your decision, and now a change flows before us. Most things that fall have the potential to break, shatter, or be destroyed. I made you as a waterfall. When it appears that you're going down, you'll simply be free-flowing or free-to-flow. Release what I've given you.

I had a procedure done in July, and for weeks after my surgery I couldn't release...no matter what or how hard I tried. I had to pray and talk to God like never before. My spiritual family held me up. They prayed and assisted me with different solutions until a release took place. In this physical release, something started changing spiritually. A release at times won't be without pain, but it will be worth it in the end. This is no different from a baby being in a pamper. The pamper was designed to hold them until a release happens resulting in "A Change" taking place. He said I can only change it once you release it!

A pamper gives way to a release however, if it's placed in water long enough it will expand. Body's of water swell or expands. He said they will see you expand right before their eyes. Release the release. Tell them once again... I can only change it once they release it!

While embracing my word, I began to hear this loud deceitful laugh. The enemy was determined to snatch my word and question my intelligence. He said doesn't the pamper expand before it's changed? Your mess will continue to get bigger before I allow a change to take place. You will be constantly weighed down by mess.

My response to him... I no longer

need the pamper. I've been potty trained. Trained to stay in Him, believe in Him, have faith in Him, and as long as I stay within Him and He in I…an expansion will take place. I've been released to be a release. Once again, He can only change it once you release it.

MONEE' SPEAKS,
A SPOKEN WORD, SPEAKING WORD

Self-Esteem

MONEE' SPEAKS,
A SPOKEN WORD, SPEAKING WORD

"Self-Esteem"

As a little one, they ask what do you want to be? In your tiny little voice, you respond, "Just like you Mommy". This is the first push to your child's dream. Though the dream may change, your support helps build their self-esteem. Oh, but not me...

When you've been molded to fit into someone else's frame...all while struggling to live up to their standards...only to realize they've never known you, just your name. Even with 99.9% DNA, the results are still the same, but that's not the sad part. When you look into the mirror, whose identity will you claim?

Raised to be a non-factor. Taught to exist instead of live...you're at a low. Where do you pull from? Where do you go? Unable to speak upon that which you feel..screaming on the inside, this *pain is deep! You need help for real...though you're a writer, pen and paper just aren't enough to help you heal.*

I need to take you all the way back before I allow you to move forward. That seed has been deeply rooted, growing, and is still being watered. You can't explain your emotions because you don't know where they've come from. All of a sudden, you felt something. Anger, rage, sadness...abandonment. Yep, there goes another one. Happiness for you has always been for a moment...you blink too hard, and it was over.

Weeks of this awkward paralyzing feeling...still can't verbalize what you're truly feeling. Praises from others are hard because the heart can't receive what the mind won't believe. Some asked why you're distant? I put space there...itching ears and flapping tongues...you only need those that really care.

What's the purpose of getting a yearly eye exam and a new prescription if you're going to wear the old glasses with limited vision? You don't understand, but self has a lot to do with what's bothering you. If I asked what's the greatest gift I gave you, I'm sure you'd say My Son. That would be true. I also gave you...the gift of you. Be not confused... self-esteem is a personal gift that I gave you. Confidence in one's own worth or abilities. I'm your Creator, it's inside of you...no matter what's been said. I esteem you.

Self-esteem is a tricky thing. Most think that the inner building up of this comes from other's...and sometimes can, but the vital nutrient can't always come from man...because

MONEE' SPEAKS,
A SPOKEN WORD, SPEAKING WORD

what's in you to build yourself up has always been a part of My plan. I didn't give you their esteem, his esteem, her esteem...you can't always rely on others words. That's why it's called SELF ESTEEM. Give yourself the gift that others tried to tear apart.

MONEE' SPEAKS,
A SPOKEN WORD, SPEAKING WORD

Self-Identity

MONEE' SPEAKS,
A SPOKEN WORD, SPEAKING WORD
"Self-Identity"

Have you ever been in a situation that you didn't speak upon yet, you became collateral damage? What was said was facts or the truth; it just didn't come by way of you. You realize you got the means to prove what was said, yet God says do nothing and remain quiet? Do what? God, I can prove this. I'm tired of the lies, the character assassination. It's been going on too long, and the proof is right here. You find yourself trying to bargain with God, though He's given you instructions. He allows you to go on and on because bottom line is He said what He said...so that's it, and that's all.

As the situation escalates, so does your desire to prove that you're right. How many of us know that you can be right and wrong at the same time? One

MONEE' SPEAKS,
A SPOKEN WORD, SPEAKING WORD

of the hardest things to do is to remain quiet when you know you're right but have been wronged. I began to say God, I need you. Help me to understand. I'm trying to remain quiet. He said Daughter, My Word says if you answer a (respond to) fool, you'll become one. Trust Me and remain quiet.

I've told you that I'm coming to deal with the bloodline witches and those that stand with them. Remain quiet. With tears streaming, all I could say was...God, I'm listening. He said you were attacked; however your identity wasn't revealed, and others chose to self-identify despite names being omitted. I waited to see if you'd respond, and you didn't. Shots fired towards you, but the bullet hit and identified the enemy. It's exposure time. I'm the Game Master, and it's time to play. See this platform of desired attention cause them to reveal the very thing they wanted to remain hidden, and that was the truth. Truth will always trigger the enemy to self-identify in an attempt to keep the lie going.

Silence at times, can kill your witness, in this case, it spoke volumes that the enemy couldn't interpret. You remained blameless because you remained quiet as instructed. When you understand it's His identity that you represent, His being that's intertwined within yours... He'll speak on your behalf. You won't have to self-identify. He'll do it for you.

Spiritual Sepsis

MONEE' SPEAKS,
A SPOKEN WORD, SPEAKING WORD

"Spiritual Sepsis"

Spiritual sepsis.....How did this enter the body? Sepsis happens when an infection you already have triggers a chain reaction throughout the body. A simple cut can become a matter of life or death instantly. Just as in the natural a tearing down or a degrading of one's being....an ungodly word or actions...an infected cut! The root of this issue may not be you...remember this infection is already in the body (in the family). No one has dealt with the generational curses, and when we're triggered, we proceed with the domino effect of tainted blood. Spiritual sepsis.

See, we come to church, and as the vessel of the hour brings forth the word, we shout out things like ok, "Pastor, you're in the vein." Now, if you took heed to what you just said, are you willing to allow God to insert *the IV? Remember you just said Pastor was in the vein! Are you willing to take the antibiotics, or are you going anti against Christ? Anti means to be opposed or against...Or are you going to keep the infection because this is what you were taught or because this is what was done to you? Spiritual sepsis.*

Just because it was in your bloodline doesn't mean it has to remain in your blood down the line. You have a choice to continue in the footsteps of those of the past or create a new path of healing for yourself and your seed(s). You get to decide when and where the generational curses end and the generational blessings begin. The choice is yours, sepsis or asepsis (absence of infection); Choice wisely.

The Chase

MONEE' SPEAKS,
A SPOKEN WORD, SPEAKING WORD

"The Chase"

I seem to be your last resort, your last option, your last choice. When the bills are paid...you don't need Me. When the results come back, and they're negative...you don't need Me. As long as your man is providing, you don't need Me. When all is going well, you don't need Me.

Now that the tables are turned...your physical man has become physical with you. Not only has he bruised your flesh, he's trying to damage your soul. Your actions towards Me are the very words he whispers in your ear. I don't need you. You forgot about the last test you took. Phone rings, and the voice on the other end says you have HIV. Broken by his actions, living in fear of his words, your life has stopped.

Though your physical being is

MONEE' SPEAKS,
A SPOKEN WORD, SPEAKING WORD

still alive, your spiritual being has completely died. You scream God, why me?! He doesn't reply. You scream again, still no answer. You begin to blame God for the choices YOU'VE made, but this time He stops you.

Wait a minute, my child, your debts I've paid. I've been trying to talk to you, but you turned a deaf ear. I tried to hold and embrace your heart, but you were too busy giving out your most precious parts. I've tried to be intimate with your mind, body & soul. I even provided a book of intimate love letters for your eyes to behold. I gave you choices; you chose him over Me. You created this soul tie and have the nerve to blame Me?

I'm the last thing you think about, but I become the first when man has failed you. Did you stop to reflect or even consider that it was I who took nails for you? See I have no desire to cause you any harm, but that brother with the six pack, chiseled face & muscular arms..yeah. The chase for him was risky, and it came at a high price. You were drawn away by your own lust. You have a habit of chasing, and too often, you sing the song I'm Chasing After You and never stop to realize that I'm in the same place YOU LEFT ME.

So, my child, before you place blame...realize that this chase was unnecessary. To chase would imply that I'm running. I said, "seek, and ye shall find."

The Conversation

MONEE' SPEAKS,
A SPOKEN WORD, SPEAKING WORD

"The Conversation"

God, I need to talk to you. I just don't understand. God, why? My child those tears aren't due to a trial or tribulation I set in place. Even though you made this decision, I still showed you grace.

God huh? I'm not understanding. If this isn't from You, then tell me what's Satan planning?! The enemy can't plan anything that I've not pre-approved, and again I tell you this outcome was all because of you.

Because of me? How is this my fault? Yes, because of you. I'm a gentleman. I don't overstep or violate your decisions, and I only come once I've been invited in. When I stood at the door of your heart, you slammed it in My face, and separate ways, we did part. What I wanted for you didn't matter. You saw/did what you *wanted, and now your heart is shattered. Without Me, it's impossible to win. You followed your flesh. Welcome to your den of sin.*

God wait! How do I correct this? Is it too late? It was only one mistake! So, you think that this is ok because it was only one mistake? My child, you have siblings dead and in graves all because of one lonely mistake. They too thought that they had time, dead and gone, and yet the clock didn't rewind.

God, is this my end? Am I out of time? This isn't the end of your life, but it could be the end of this chapter. Again, that decision is yours to make. Choose wisely. Life is filled with costly mistakes. God, I'm sorry. Please forgive me. My child, the moment you asked, I forgave and said be it unto thee.

The Garment

MONEE' SPEAKS,
A SPOKEN WORD, SPEAKING WORD
"The Garment"

Have you ever heard the phrase you're slayed to the Gods? Hair, nails, make-up, and clothes on point, but let me ask you a question. Can you slay a demon? You're looking at me all crossed-eyed because I'm not a label whore. Yeah, you have on red bottoms just to impress him. I just want to touch the hem. The hem of His garment that is. We are cut from two different cloths. Sis, you're materialistic. What I'm clothed in can't be bought.

Righteousness, dignity, and strength clothe me. This temple belongs to the one who covers me. Ya see, Sis I'm a thick chic. Even my shapewear is anointed because I understand that it should be just as powerful as the armor.

Again, The Armor of God, that is.

MONEE' SPEAKS,
A SPOKEN WORD, SPEAKING WORD

Tight fitting...intended to smooth, control and shape my destiny. Nothing will jiggle in or out of the spirit. It's not always about what you're wearing but more so about what's wearing you down. Even on my heaviest day, I'm still lighter than you because the garments I wear have been tried, tested, and proven to be true.

Who Am I?

MONEE' SPEAKS,
A SPOKEN WORD, SPEAKING WORD
"Who Am I?"

At one point, I thought I knew. A case of mistaken identity, yeah, that's definitely true. I wasn't encouraged to be all that I could be. Instead, I was told that I was beneath man, and no one would ever want me, not even God, you see.

In school, they teach you that words have power. Power, you say? Maybe they can help me... I built up the nerve and decided to talk. Mrs.J, can I tell you something?. This is the second time, and even he said it was my fault. Her reply... Get away from me. I don't have time. You're mean, rebellious, and how do I know this isn't a lie? A lie?! Really?! There's that voice again "I told you no one is going to help you. You're only allowed to do and be what I tell you".

At 12, I had no one and nothing left to believe in. The school system had failed me. I tried to do something new and confide because I was sick of the hurt, pain, and lies. Where do I turn now? Again, the suicide demon crept up. I took every pill that I could find that night. They were taking too long and making me sick. I didn't want to feel I just wanted it to end quick.

Determined that my life was about to expire, and pills weren't enough. Slicing my wrist again wasn't an option since it didn't work the first time. With intense stomach pain from the pills, I still refused to give up. I was yet determined, and my mind was made up. I decided to drink bleach. It literally felt like fire was shut up in my bones! This was the first time I heard a different voice say.. Do as you will, but My will, will be done.

You're looking at a miracle because I allowed satan to convince me that by this time tomorrow, 6 ft under at the *age of 12 in my grave I would be.*

I cried and moaned in pain all night. I couldn't tell anyone what I did because I knew they didn't care and probably would've assisted in my death. This was also the first time a voice tried to comfort me. It took a weak insecure man to break you. He took what wasn't rightfully his, but I am The Man that can restore and definitely heal. Though I heard the words I couldn't receive because of all of the pain by the age of 12 in God, I don't believe.

My granny took us to church, and the preacher said God would save you. I got angry and said he's full of lies because what God would allow a man to come in and rape you? Like most churches I've experienced they turned a deaf ear. Acted as if I said nothing. Ushered me to sit down and to stop being disrespectful. My granny sat as if she was deaf and blind. She didn't even turn towards me as I stood there crying. Never did I return. Church was no different from home, when I did go, I was still alone.

Years went by, and I'd completely given up on life. I heard that voice again out of nowhere, "Don't give up, give Me another try. I'm sending you someone that will speak life". That gift I did receive. If you ask me, who am I? I will stand and declare that I'm the woman God created me to be.

MONEE' SPEAKS,
A SPOKEN WORD, SPEAKING WORD

Worth

MONEE' SPEAKS,
A SPOKEN WORD, SPEAKING WORD

"Worth"

"Minimizing Your Worth"

Are you being treated as an Heir? Like royalty, or are you being treated or referenced as the measurement size of a mattress? Hmmm, not following me?

Ok..so you say he's your King, and you're his Queen... Right? There's no covenant between the two of you. What's separating you from Me is the very thing that's causing you two to be attached to one another.

Kings and Queens are royal titles...to be used with capital letters, not lower-case letters referring to your bed size. When done, you only end up feeling used.

Ask him if he's truly desiring to be your King or just desiring to have you in his king-size bed? You are only his queen when you're lying flat on your back in your queen-size bed.

Actions completed, and you go back to being whatever your parents named you. Never realizing that you're worth having MRS. before your name....

Never realizing she's worth having your last name. See for every King, I created a Queen. Sir, you want a title and to be treated as "head of household?" Why when you can't even hold down a job? Always comparing her to your mother and grandmother. How they were the helpmates to their partners but are you doing what your father and grandfather did to reap those benefits? Nah, you don't want a help mate; you just want to help make her life miserable.

Ma'am, do you not understand your worth? Why have a peasant mentality when you came from royalty? It's not his responsibility to show you your worth. How can he? Don't expect him to operate or carry a title for a position that he's unqualified for... But what he is doing...is treating you as you treat yourself?

You gave him permission to do so by minimizing your own worth. You don't appreciate the value of your being...so your soul is being depreciated... Oh, and by the way, you're not the only one he's seeing!

Stop being a happy meal when I created you to be soul food. A piece of anything, in most cases, isn't a sign of peace. Don't just be a queen by way of a mattress.

Detox your temple. Release him so you can be free. There's nothing wrong with Miss or Ms. before your name. Walk in the status of a Princess until your true King comes along, stands before God, and legally changes your last name. He'll be aware and willing to put in the work. That three-strand cord...You, Him, and God....just maximized your worth.

WAYS TO CONNECT WITH MONEE' REASE

For Spoken Word Engagements
Contact by

Email: Moneespeaks@gmail.com

or

Facebook page: Monee' Speaks

MONEE' SPEAKS, A SPOKEN WORD, SPEAKING WORD

Made in the USA
Columbia, SC
23 May 2024